Inspiration

AFRICAN
VOICES

Poetry & Tales

Publisher and Creative Director: Nick Wells
Senior Project Editor: Josie Mitchell
Art Director and Layout Design: Mike Spender
Digital Design and Production: Chris Herbert

Special thanks to Badilisha Poetry X-Change and the Africa Centre, which provide
an outlet for thousands of Pan-African poets to reach new audiences and archive
these important voices. badilishapoetry.com | africacentre.net

FLAME TREE PUBLISHING
6 Melbray Mews
London SW6 3NS
United Kingdom

www.flametreepublishing.com
First published 2019

19 21 23 22 20
1 3 5 7 9 10 8 6 4 2

A CIP record for this book is available from the British Library upon request.

ISBN 978-1-78755-306-4

Printed in China | Created, Developed & Produced in the United Kingdom

Inspiration

AFRICAN VOICES

Poetry & Tales

Introduction by
Wanjiru Koinange

FLAME TREE
PUBLISHING

CONTENTS

INTRODUCTION

Reader, welcome. You have quite the poetic journey ahead of you.

It's an incredible honour to have the work of 19 Badilisha poets featured in this collection.

Badilisha Poetry X-Change is the largest online audio archive of African Poetry on the planet, a programme run by the Africa Centre. At inception ten years ago, Badilisha was a poetry festival that took place in South Africa. After three years of running the festival, we made the shift into an online poetry channel because we believed that it was the only way to provide an outlet for the thousands of Pan-African poets to reach new audiences and to archive these important voices. Badilisha was the first internet-based channel dedicated exclusively to the poets of Africa and its diaspora.

The diversity of voice, dialect and language that lives on the African continent is truly incredible. Badilisha has archived close to 700 poets from 34 countries but this merely scratches the surface of a continent whose citizens are exposed to oral and literary traditions almost as soon as they can speak. Kenya, for instance, is a country with over 40 tribes, each with its own distinct set of traditions that are more a way of life than performance. Traditionally, proverbs would be exchanged as greetings and riddles were used to solve disputes. On the East African coast in Kangas, colourful rectangular pieces of fabric that bore a *methali* (proverb) on the bottom border, were used by women to deliver delicate messages. With time our poetry became a means to speak to our encounters with slavery, colonization and segregation. Many African writers who did speak out against these powers ended up in detention or exile, so fear sealed the lips of countless others. Freedom of expression is still curtailed in many parts of the continent, but still, as you will soon discover, poetry prevails.

Explorations of place, culture, womanhood, inner life, joy and identity become alive on the pages of this anthology. Poets offer praise, introspection, celebration and fresh perspective. You will dance in Tanzania, and then your legs will mourn with Kafoi Gbewonyo. Vignettes on exile sit eloquent alongside essays on liberty. Notable literary voices such as Yewande Omotoso, Tjawangwa Dema and academic Tiro Sebina nestle the emerging expressions of Tina Abena Oforiwa and Mariska Taylor-Darko. The rediscovery of poets such as Nana Asma'u and Eugène Marais are truly a delight and will be a gift to all lovers of words.

Consider this collection an invitation to explore the wealth of poetic voices available out there: via Badilisha, through anthologies, magazines, poetry gatherings and other groundbreaking platforms. Many poets you will encounter here are responsible for building organizations that showcase poetry in distinct ways. Adjei Agyei Baah, for instance, is a founder of the Poetry Foundation in Ghana. Gloria D. Gonsalves has been plugged into Tanzania's poetry landscape for years.

Based in Cape Town, the Africa Centre works to support and highlight the work of Africans who are engaged in transforming the widespread, incomplete and myopic narratives about the continent. The poetry in this book is only a small sample of the poems in its Badilisha Poetry X-Change archives and African poetry from throughout history, but it is our hope that everyone who reads this collection discovers something new about our deeply layered continent. Happy reading.

Wanjiru Koinange
badilishapoetry.com | africacentre.net

Wanjiru Koinange is a Kenyan writer. Her debut novel *The Havoc of Choice* will be published worldwide in July 2019. She also manages three programs at the Africa Centre – Badilisha Poetry X-Change, Artists in Residency and Talking Heads. These programs all explore ways in which artistic production can influence social change. She is a co-founder of Book Bunk, a social impact firm that exists to restore old libraries, and install new ones, into public spaces in Nairobi.

RISING
VOICES

That's All

Gold
blue
veld
sky;
and one bird wheeling lonely, high—
that's all.

An exile come back
from over the sea;
a grave in the grass,
a tear breaking free;
    that's all.

Jan F.E. Celliers (1865–1940)

NEON POEM

after Amiri Baraka's 'Black Art'

Poems are bullshit
unless they teach.
Poems serve no purpose
unless they reach
the audience they are written for,
the ears they are meant for.

You could write the perfect love poem,
tell us how you teased her
till she let you touch her,
but if she cannot remember you,
then, sir, your poetry didn't do what it was supposed to.

I've heard war poems
that hid behind fancy syllables and metaphors,
quietly comfortable with the thought of coming to blows
over why they should fight for anything at all.

Once, I wrote a hope poem,
one of those *there is a future–type* poems,
but it never spoke
till what few wishes we had left broke.

I've even seen live poems
that wait till the audience is gone
then begin humming softly as a song,
murdering any sense of rhythm they might have had at all.
I'm thinking of an *it's too late* poem.
I'll build it up till it sounds like metal bats against tin cans,
Loud and outrageous, still too little too late.

We want fast poems
that can outrace us, outface us,
maybe even take us to where we've never been,
quick as sin.

A *look at me* poem
that screams out to the world,
"Open up your eyes and see,
you can't even speak your mind,
yet you still believe that you and you
and we are free
from something or someone."

Anyone, give me a neon poem:
a black, red, white, yellow, purple, pink, even lime poem
that will teach all other wannabe poems
how to grow up and become real type poems,
because poems are bullshit
unless they teach;
they serve absolutely no purpose
unless they reach
someone.

Tjawangwa Dema

A Haughty Woman

My wide hips dance
to melodious tones
of my tight thighs.
I am a soprano
of unique creation.

My lips sing
a song of praise
about a mouth
whose thick flesh
I naturally possess.

My chest comforts
young and old
as they weep hard
on soft wellness
of my big twos.

I possess not
the imposed numbers
86-61-86
but look a lot sexier
in my natural curves.

Oh!
Look at you
feeling all upset
about my pride.
Try be yourself.

Gloria D. Gonsalves

Televised Revolution

This revolution will be televised for their evolution
    needs to be revised
Because we are victims of a revelation that was
    contrived

I sit on the threshold as I behold a party of pilgrims
    from across the bridge
Their bodies frozen cold as a fridge
We revolutionaries sit on the edge of pain like cow
    dung on farm ridge
Like black butterflies blown by contrary winds and ditched
Hope and anger linger together hook line and sinker like
    tuna about to be fished
Their intelligence make me want to say ish
What do they think you are
Tell me
A foolish young village belle looking to be hitched?
Ish
Again then, I am but an extension of my pen
An expression of my pain

I am saying

My revolution will be televised

Because I possess a revelation that needs not to be revised

We are being threatened by theories of evolution that
    was foolishly contrived

We suffer as if by electrocution

That's how our souls are bein sensitised

The powers that seem to be deem to only have
    our minds lobotomised

Automation by evolution's proponents is the goal
    of this counter revolution and its pungent

These people are mere agents of an unknown civilisation

And as you get older you get colder

In your pseudo life of a soldier

You look like a washed out

Washed thru

Washed up

Washed in

Has been

That's been

Living

In a bin

Living on gin and cigarette filters

Filthy

Feeling guilty

Cos yo failure is your monument

You fail to grasp your moment

You are an orchid set in cement

Blaming everyone else but yourself for your up

    ending internment

Free yourself from prison

The prisms of your ego

Be like me

Fight the system that be

Can't you see

You are valued less than they value a tree

Screw your civility

What is civil about a war

That's not a revolution

That's your evolution of evil

The madness of a people gone ill

Symptomatic of the hand of the devil

Why do you want to rise and kill
That's ill
Yet still
My revolution must be televised
My people must be sensitised
This reality should no longer be romanticised
No need too late to apologise

Have you seen icy tears slither from a cold heart thru
    eyes not there
Have you felt pain you couldn't shed a tear
Have you had fright you couldn't shudder in fear
Has apathy hit you like a zulu spear
As reason and emotion morph none any longer clear
And yet you arch to hear
The word in your ear
Visions and appaeitions spoken by this seer
And if its true that life's best are free
Why is free this dear
The drumbeat of this revolution draws near
And this revolution must be televised
And even if my revolution was contrived

The evolution of my revolution is so every man woman
      boy and girl can
truly claim we are free
Do you agree

Sage Hassan

WINTERNAG (EXTRACT)

O cold is the thin wind
    And sere.
And bright in the twilight
    And bare,
as wide as the mercy of God
lies the veld in starlight and shadow.
    And high on the ridges
    Scattered in scorched earth,
the grass ears are nodding
    like beckoning hands.
The tune of the east wind,
    melancholy measure,
sings the song of a maiden
forlorn of her lover.
In the fold of each grass
shines a droplet of dew,
and quickly it whitens
to frost in the cold!

Eugène Marais (1871–1936)

LIBERATION

All I want is to be free/the liberation of me
To be released from the prison
That he fashioned for my bondage
After illegally occupying the mansion that houses my spirit
He would go about desecrating my temple
Profaning the sacredness of my body's internal
Abusing my vessel
Blocking my channel to the light at the end of the tunnel
Keeping me in darkness
Emphasizing my weakness/flaunting his mistress
Damaging my esteem and my being to the point
That I felt powerless
In the name of love I let myself be violated by a narcissist
A terrorist in romantic disguise
He would constantly bomb my body and attack my mind
He would offer me up as a ritual sacrifice at the altar
    of his ego
To make himself feel macho
Bombing my body/attacking my mind
He waged an unholy war/on everything my womanhood
    stood for

He was obviously on a mission to reduce me to rubble

Using supreme cruelty and extreme brutality

To induce me to crumble

Sometimes his tactics were subtle

But always designed to leave me feeling very unstable

It was exploitation at the highest level

But it was only possible as long as I stayed ignorant

So it's no surprise the day this sister achieved enlightenment

Was the same day I began to see visions of freedom

To imagine the reality of a life free from his torture

Daydreams of reclaiming my stolen royalty

Loving myself in totality

Erasing his mistreatment of my beauty

from the sanctuary of memory

Celebrating the infinite power of me

Now strong enough to defend myself from any future
    attacks of the enemy

Because all I want is to be free

The liberation of me

Cynthia 'Flowchyld' Marangwanda

In the House of Exile

This town I have adopted
Snoops at me suspiciously
Veiled in the colour of its skin
Blind to my dark presence
Only the green of nature
Breathes out clean air
I look homeward and see no angels
Heol Pentremeurig is too narrow a road
As parked cars crowd the street of my life
Perhaps exile is only skin deep
Memories of home time will confiscate
The deep-freeze of history
This town I have adopted
Cobbled streets, here, everywhere
Is the masonry of centuries past and
The search draws me nowhere
Near kindred spirits
In this town I have adopted
"I'm the incredulous sneer
tucked beneath bland smiles."

Tinashe Mushakavanhu

Higher Learning

I can't explain why my father left.
I remember the mug in the kitchen filled
with half a cup of coffee, an ash tray with
half a Marlboro stick, its fumes still lingering.

Weeks after he was gone his CK cologne
could be smelt everywhere on everything,
reeking of his absence.

Mum took to knitting on Mondays,
Bible study on Tuesdays and on all the
other days would sit in the darkness
the light from the TV flickering,
at times refracting her loneliness.

In this land, he could leave.
Her dark hue was no longer beautiful
the weight of her love was breaking his back.
But Oh, what about Accra?

Or the nights in Kumasi making love to
Fella's blues?

Over the static line her sisters pray, curse,
dissect his reasoning, repeat in three different
languages that she wasn't to blame.

"He is a man and men leave," they say.

Our ears pressed behind the door we ate those
words didn't we?

That Monday your teacher asked about our father,
apologised in a monotone way that these things
happen and you aren't to blame.
You regurgitated the knowledge you had acquired
That "he is a man, and men leave."

Tina Abena Oforiwa

By Your Side

The cock crows at 5 a.m. You were up since 4 listening to the silence. You know soon this will be a thing of the past. You're a pair of sardines in a tin; she taps your leg and whispers 'Maabena, are you awake?' You nod, staring up at the concrete ceiling. It rained last night. You fell asleep listening to the pitter patter of water falling on the iron sheet, and to her, snoring beside you.

Your aunt is up singing along with the cassette, the wondering love songs of Daddy Lumba going on about how dangerous women are; you hear your father grunt his approval. Afia is the first to hit the shower. Since she has grown breast the size of pebbles she now sings about love. As for you two, love is found in bowls of maize porridge and fried doughnuts, you don't speak of the impending departure.

Soon you are out on the veranda in the shade. The sun lapping up against the concrete. She jumps in and jumps out, thrusts her hands towards the sky, right then someone takes a picture. The picture you will later carry like a passport in your purse. She will always look free, and you, looking in at her freedom.

She will smile more, laugh harder and you will wonder how? London couldn't teach you to reach for the sun, but all the while she had it buried within her skin, her dark hue testifies to this. Years later you will kiss her palms and pray into her hands and she will laugh. Never understanding that akwaaba was the scent of her fingers greeting your face, a gentle reminder that this, is home.

Tina Abena Oforiwa

THE DEATH WISH

Sometimes I wish for being a wife
and having children to take to soccer practice.
Being a bored housewife with a more bored husband;
a man who sneaks to find sex somewhere wetter,
        more dangerous.
I wish for this.

For shopping lists with shaving cream at the top and
'Honey, I need new vests'.
I wish for this, for an accustomed-to dullness,
instead of holding my breath all the time,
hoping for magic,
hoping to be touched, be adored.

I want something usual. And regular. And broken.
I want my fairy tale splayed in front of me, begging
        but bleeding.
I want to arrive in the land of the settled,
distracted by money. Numbed.

It's the closest thing to dying without having to be buried.
And sometimes I wish for this.

Yewande Omotoso

RISE

At times I feel stuck in this place called the Cape Flats
My mental's enchained, engraved in these streets
Where people roam, constantly dragging our feet,
No one to believe in what we are selling,
Yet we keep on buying and buying these lies
    and artificial living
Teach us to teach and learn our nations lessons
Motivate us with our own experience
So we can Feel again, Breathe again, Believe &
Rise like never before…

For, we're a people with history,
Roots, deeply rooted, we need to search for it
Not just any story, prescribed and printed with lies
Stories known and alive, with truth in it
So true, we can feel the life in it,
See the light in the sense it makes,
The time to awake is not tomorrow, it's today
Where I can be taught & see the light
Guiding my way, toward, the path where my ancestors wait…

To fill me and Bless me, so I can clearly see,

My truth at last…

Rise!

Janine 'Blaq Pearl' Van Rooy-Overmeyer

FORGIVE AND FORGET

A green and growing thorn-tree
stood right against the track
where long spans of oxen
passed to the north and back.

But one day as it grew there
a wagon rode it down,
the big wheels cut a pathway
across the bright green crown.

The wagon rolling onward
was gone behind the hill;
slowly the thorn came upright,
slowly by its own will.

Its loveliness was shattered,
its young bark broken through;
one place the sapling body
was nearly cut in two.

But slowly, surely upright
the stricken tree has come,
and healed its wounds by dropping
the balm of its own gum.

In course of time the hurt-marks
fade where the wheels had lunged –
only one place endures
that cannot be expunged.

The wounds grew healed and healthy,
with years that come and go,
but that one scar grew greater
and does not cease to grow.

Totius (1877–1953)

MOTHER'S TOUCH

In the village compound which was cleanly swept and tidy,
a compound not easily accessible by road,
a group of old women sat huddled together.
Sticks and pipes jutted out of their mouths
which occasionally moved in unison.
A sigh here, a look up to the sky there.
Some sat with their chins in their palms.
They spoke.

This is the time that I should be with my sons
    and their wives,
with my daughters, and their husbands.
My children should be looking after me now,
after all the blood, sweat and tears that I shed
    for many days and nights
in their time of illness, their time of pain,
    their time of sorrow.

I felt pain when they were born
but it was such sweet pain when I looked into the
    faces of the new life that I had given,

I felt joy when they were growing up and happiness
      when they became adults,
I felt pain when they left home to set up their new lives
but joy when they came to visit, sitting and laughing
while they enjoyed their mother's cooking.
I felt pain when they were going through difficulties,
but joy when they overcame their hurdles

Now I sit alone, some stranger, a prophet,
      in the name of religion,
put their struggles and problems on my head –
"Your mother is a witch, she wants
      to destroy you"

Just because I am old, a widow, helpless and defenseless,
just because my poverty and suffering is drawn on my face,
I am the scourge of my village.

Would I destroy my life? Life that came
      out from me?
I may have lost my youth but not my mind.

Now I don't see my children, don't know some
    of my grandchildren,
my husband's family doesn't remember me.

There is a pain that never goes, it just stays there in the
heart, in the womb and gradually eats away at life
    itself – oh the pain.
Old men don't get called witches,
they just marry younger women and continue with life.
What is it that women do wrong in their lives?
Maybe they love and care too much,
maybe they sacrifice too much,
feel too much.

When I die it will be too late for anyone to say "I am sorry,"
But I continue to love my children,
I continue to feel them in my arms,
I continue to see their laughter and joy,
I continue to live for the day when I would be called
"Maame" again –
oh the pain.

One day, someone somewhere will weep,
because they can no longer get back that mother's touch,
that mother's love, that mother's smile –
oh the pain.

Mariska Taylor-Darko

To Young South Africa (extract)

Lo! a dream-shape in the distance beckoning on
    to nobler deeds:
Up, my brethren, rise and follow where the
    star-wreathed vision leads;
Leave your toil of fruitless labour, vainly with
    o'er-weared hands
Weaving aye your web of fortune from the
    dull earth's yellow sands,
Striving with your lofty talents to enslave
    yourselves to clay,
Chaining spirits born for ages to the task-work of a day.

Toil! – but not for wasteful nothings; toil! – but not
    for self alone;
This it is "for ever rolling upwards still the rolling stone";
This is the curse of Eden, still bequeathed from man to man:
"Strive but vainly,—work and gain not," echoing aye the
    angel's ban.
Yet upon this curse a blessing when the god-like
    human will
Moulds it unto glorious purpose, and doth hallow all the ill!

Never sainted prophet stricken prostrate on the
    burning sod,

Trembling 'neath the awful glory streaming from
    the present God,

Heard in earthquake, flame, or stillness, aught more
    holy than the truth

Echoed by our mother Nature from her dawn of early youth

Through all ages – "Man is God-like – weak and erring,
    suffering man,

God-like in the thoughts of the thinketh, God-like in
    the deeds he can."

Yea! and with the curse upon him, more he proves
    his lofty birth

Than in yon old Eden dwelling, sated with the ease of earth,

When he strives for men around him, battles for his
    brother's right;

When he spreads amid the darkest rays of never-dying
    light—

Rays that calmly shining from him reach the weary
    sufferer's breast,

Warm once more the frozen feelings, bringing
    ease to his unrest;
Rays whose widely beaming brilliance shows all men one
    brotherhood,
Man then only rightly human when he yearns for
    human good.

Mighty nations then most glorious when their world-wide
    cherished name
Is a succor to the helpless, unto tyrants fear and shame!
When their deeds have been of justice, mercies done and
    wisdom spread,
Waking noble aspirations where the human soul
    seemed dead;
God-like then is human labour: brethren rend'ring
    brethren blest,
Feel themselves divinely nurtured, know a God within
    their breast.

Anon.

SONNET

I leant my breast against the golden gate
That bars the body from the land of dreams,
But lets the soul to roam in lawns where wait
Or wander down the banks of shining streams
The dead and living, holding strange debate
Of things that yet should happen 'neath the beams
Of suns as yet unrisen, whilst listless Fate
Paused, and the stars unyoked their tired teams.

And as my hand the latch sought, for I fain
Had followed one who wore a white rose-wreath,
Sleep touched mine eyes with darkness, and the pain
Of longing ceased; and when I next drew breath
I heard a voice low whisper, "It is vain
To enter here – thou first must drink of death!"

W.C. Scully

GODS &
ANCESTORS

ASHANTI

The edenic garden on a fertile land of gold
Ashanti!

The kingdom whose boundaries were only penetrated
With treaties never with canons
Ashanti!

The empire whose monarchy was furiously fissured
Yet could not be humbled into crumbs
Ashanti!

The people whose culture and tradition
Is a feast of smiling stars in their sparkling splendour
Ashantis!

The kingdom whose majestic steps
Always tame the troubled waters
Ashanti!

The empire blessed by the gods with a stool of gold
Ashanti!

The first graduates of Ananse's weaving school[1]
Ashanti!

The people whose hospitality
Turns strangers into natives
Ashanti!

The empire whose installation of her kings
Make the whole world walk to Manhyia[2]
Ashanti!

The people whose heads are held high
Under the legendary leadership of Osei Tutu[3]
Ashanti!

The porcupine warriors
Who double in thousands with the last man standing
Ashantis!

The porcupine warriors
Who never run out of quills!

Adjei Agyei-Baah

FOOTNOTES

1. *Ananse*: In West African folktales, a popular spider
   god who is both devious and very wise.

2. *Manhyia*: A town which serves as the seat of Ashanti
   Kingdom, housing the Manhyia Palace (i.e. The Ashanti
   Kings Palace) and Ashanti Museum.

3. *Osei Tutu*: Osei Tutu I was the founder of the Empire of
   Asante. Otumfuo Osei Tutu II is the current traditional
   ruler of the Kingdom of Ashanti.

Inheritance

Motho ga a itsiwe e se naga[1]
— *Setswana proverb*

children know everything is a forest
    they think of men as stories
open their faces to each passerby
    as they do to the thick-knee's warble
at the end of childhood they'll not ask
    they'll take what they know from learning
what comes of their blood-bright coats
    flickering in the woods
a small growl squatting on evening wind

even their father who turns his blank face
    into their song
is a forest
    children learn its woodland ways
to lie on bare floors prostrating
    until the wolf is gone
they learn to hear his foot's tenor
    twigs snapping away beyond the eye

at night
    they lie awake and imagine
their mother's face opening like a child's
    waiting to be transformed
a muffled song on her lips
    not much to it
they'll be wolves or they'll be men

turn to prophecy and devour their mother

or castrate their father while he sleeps

Tjawangwa Dema

FOOTNOTE

1.   Translation: 'A person is unknowable
    because they are not a forest'.

The Pure in Heart Shall See God

They shall see Him in the crimson flush
    Of morning's early light,
In the drapery of sunset,
    Around the couch of night.
When the clouds drop down their fatness,
    In late and early rain,
They shall see His glorious footprints
    On valley, hill and plain.
They shall see Him when the cyclone
    Breathes terror through the land;
They shall see Him 'mid the murmurs
    Of zephyrs soft and bland.
They shall see Him when the lips of health,
    Breath vigor through each nerve,
When pestilence clasps hands with death,
    His purposes to serve.
They shall see Him when the trembling earth
    Is rocking to and fro;
They shall see Him in the order
    The seasons come and go.
They shall see Him when the storms of war

Sweep wildly through the land;
When peace descends like gentle dew
    They still shall see His hand.
They shall see Him in the city
    Of gems and pearls of light,
They shall see Him in his beauty,
    And walk with Him in white.
To living founts their feet shall tend,
    And Christ shall be their guide,
Beloved of God, their rest shall be
    In safety by His side.

Frances Harper (1825–1911)

UNTITLED

From *The Life, History, and Unparalleled Sufferings of John Jea, the African Preacher. Compiled and Written by Himself*

The love of God did me constrain,
To seek the wandering souls of men;
With cries, intreaties, tears, to save,
To snatch them from the burning blaze.

For this let man revile my name,
No cross I shun, I fear no shame;
All hail reproach and welcome shame;
Only thy terrors Lord restrain.

My life, my blood, I here present,
If for thy truth they may be spent;
Fulfil thy sovereign counsel Lord,
Thy will be done, thy name ador'd.

Give me thy strength, O God of Pow'r
Then let winds blow, or thunders roar;

Thy faithful witness will I be,
They're fixt, I can do all through thee.

John Jea (born 1773)

UNTITLED

From *The Life, History, and Unparalleled Sufferings of John Jea, the African Preacher. Compiled and Written by Himself*

I am not ashamed to own my Lord,
Nor to defend his cause;
Maintain the honour of his word,
The glory of his erose.

Jesus, my God, I know his name,
His name is all my trust;
Nor will he put my soul to shame,
Nor let my hope be lost.

Firm as his throne his promise stands,
And he can well secure,
What I have committed to his hands,
Till the decisive hour.

John Jea (born 1773)

Remembering Queen Nzinga & Young Africa

In the scowling darkness that shadowed all dreams
I met a bodacious queen
Black and brazen
She was whistling a tune
Captivating but simple
Her song refused to be packaged
It was forever creating spaces

The authority of her smile
Invited even thunder to her beck and call
Her breath commanded the mighty hawks,
Warhogs and eagles.
Her trance like war dance
amazingly soulful

From the mighty Queen Nzinga
A sharp insular spark of energy
glowed eternally
Her ocean wide mind
her vibrant laughter

contained the wisdom of a million books
Her toes scratched the earth with pride,
She was a friend of the moon
and a friend to the tiniest of insects

Trees grinned and flowers glowed
in her hallowed presence
A tested friend of life
Her healing hand amended God's mistakes
And comforted life's orphans
Her generous mind fed millions of earnest hopes
and potent dreams

Tiro Sebina

ON BEING BROUGHT FROM AFRICA TO AMERICA

'Twas mercy brought me from my Pagan land,
Taught my benighted soul to understand
That there's a God, that there's a Saviour too:
Once I redemption neither fought nor knew,
Some view our sable race with scornful eye,
"Their colour is a diabolic die."
Remember, Christians, Negroes, black as Cain,
May be refin'd, and join th' angelic train.

Phillis Wheatley (c. 1753–84)

ON RECOLLECTION

Mneme begin. Inspire, ye sacred nine,
Your vent'rous Afric in her great design.
Mneme, immortal pow'r, I trace thy spring:

Assist my strains, while I thy glories sing:

The acts of long departed years, by thee
Recover'd, in due order rang'd we see:

Thy pow'r the long-forgotten calls from night,
That sweetly plays before the fancy's sight.
Mneme in our nocturnal visions pours
The ample treasure of her secret stores;

Swift from above the wings her silent flight
Through Phoebe's realms, fair regent of the night;

And, in her pomp of images display'd,
To the high-raptur'd poet gives her aid,
Through the unbounded regions of the mind,
Diffusing light celestial and refin'd.

The heav'nly phantom paints the actions done
By ev'ry tribe beneath the rolling sun.
Mneme, enthron'd within the human breast,
Has vice condemn'd, and ev'ry virtue blest.

How sweet the sound when we her plaudit hear?
Sweeter than music to the ravish'd ear,
Sweeter than Maro's entertaining strains
Resounding through the groves, and hills, and plains.

But how is Mneme dreaded by the race,
Who scorn her warnings and despise her grace?
By her unveil'd each horrid crime appears,
Her awful hand a cup of wormwood bears.

Days, years mispent, O what a hell of woe!
Hers the worst tortures that our souls can know.

Now eighteen years their destin'd course have run,
In fast succession round the central sun.
How did the follies of that period pass

Unnotic'd, but behold them writ in brass!

In Recollection see them fresh return,
And sure 'tis mine to be asham'd, and mourn.

O Virtue, smiling in immortal green,
Do thou exert thy pow'r, and change the scene;
Be thine employ to guide my future days,
And mine to pay the tribute of my praise.

Of Recollection such the pow'r enthron'd
In ev'ry breast, and thus her pow'r is own'd.

The wretch, who dar'd the vengeance of the skies,
At last awakes in horror and surprise,
By her alarm'd, he sees impending fate,
He howls in anguish, and repents too late.

But O! what peace, what joys are hers t' impart
To ev'ry holy, ev'ry upright heart!

Thrice blest the man, who, in her sacred shrine,
Feels himself shelter'd from the wrath divine!

Phillis Wheatley (c. 1753–84)

To Maecenas

Maecenas, you, beneath the myrtle shade,
Read o'er what poets sung, and shepherds play'd.
What felt those poets but you feel the same?
Does not your soul possess the sacred flame?

Their noble strains your equal genius shares
In softer language, and diviner airs.
While Homer paints, lo! circumfus'd in air,
Celestial Gods in mortal forms appear;

Swift as they move hear each recess rebound,
Heav'n quakes, earth trembles, and the shores resound.
Great Sire of verse, before my mortal eyes,
The lightnings blaze across the vaulted skies,

And, as the thunder shakes the heav'nly plains,
A deep felt horror thrills through all my veins.
When gentler strains demand thy graceful song,
The length'ning line moves languishing along.

When great Patroclus courts Achilles' aid,

The grateful tribute of my tears is paid;
Prone on the shore he feels the pangs of love,
And stern Pelides tend'rest passions move.

Great Maro's strain in heav'nly numbers flows,
The Nine inspire, and all the bosom glows.
O could I rival thine and Virgil's page,
Or claim the Muses with the Mantuan Sage;

Soon the same beauties should my mind adorn,
And the same ardors in my soul should burn:
Then should my song in bolder notes arise,
And all my numbers pleasingly surprise;

But here I sit, and mourn a grov'ling mind,
That fain would mount, and ride upon the wind.
Not you, my friend, these plaintive strains become,
Not you, whose bosom is the Muses home;

When they from tow'ring Helicon retire,
They fan in you the bright immortal fire,

But I less happy, cannot raise the song,
The fault'ring music dies upon my tongue.

The happier Terence all the choir inspir'd,
His soul replenish'd, and his bosom fir'd;
But say, ye Muses, why this partial grace,
To one alone of Afric's sable race;

From age to age transmitting thus his name
With the finest glory in the rolls of fame?
Thy virtues, great Maecenas! shall be sung
In praise of him, from whom those virtues sprung:

While blooming wreaths around thy temples spread,
I'll snatch a laurel from thine honour'd head,
While you indulgent smile upon the deed.

As long as Thames in streams majestic flows,
Or Naiads in their oozy beds repose
While Phoebus reigns above the starry train
While bright Aurora purples o'er the main,

So long, great Sir, the muse thy praise shall sing,
So long thy praise shal' make Parnassus ring:

Then grant, Maecenas, thy paternal rays,
Hear me propitious, and defend my lays.

Phillis Wheatley (c. 1753–84)

THE YOUNG MAN AND THE SKULL

One day a young hunter had journeyed far into the bush in search of antelope when he accidentally stumbled upon a skull lying in the earth. Drawing nearer, he stooped to the ground to examine the object and began muttering to himself:

"How did you manage to get here my friend? What can have brought you to this unhappy end?"

To the young man's absolute astonishment, the skull opened its jaws and began speaking: "Talking brought me here, my friend. Talking brought me to this place." The hunter raced back towards his village to tell the people all about his discovery. "Friends," he cried excitedly, "I have just come across a human skull in the bush and it has spoken to me. It must be a wonderful sign.

"Nonsense," they replied, "how can you possibly hold a conversation with the head of a dead man?" "But it really did speak to me," the young man insisted, "you only refuse to believe me because you are jealous." But still the people continued to jeer him. "Why not go and tell the chief all about your discovery," one mocked, "I'm sure he'll be overjoyed by the news!" "I will do precisely that," retorted the young man angrily, and off he marched towards the chief's house to tell him all about the skull.

But the chief, who had been taking his afternoon nap, was extremely unhappy that he had been disturbed.
"Why have you come here with your tall stories?" he shouted. "You had better be telling the truth or I will see to it that your own head comes off. Now, take me to this wretched place and let me hear the skull's message for myself."

A small crowd set off from the village, arriving shortly afterwards at the place where the young man had made his discovery. And sure enough, they soon spotted the skull sitting in the earth.

"It looks perfectly ordinary," complained the people after a time, "when are we going to hear it speak?"

The young man crouched to the ground and repeated the words he had first spoken to the skull. But no answer came and the skull's jaws remained firmly shut. Again, the hunter spoke to it, raising his voice more loudly, but only silence followed.

Now the crowd began to grow restless and when a third and fourth attempt produced exactly the same result, they leapt on the young man and chopped off his head as the chief had ordered.

The head fell to the ground and rolled alongside the skull. For a long time afterwards all remained quiet as the villagers disappeared over the hill bearing the body homewards for burial. Then the skull opened its jaws and spoke up: "How did you manage to get here my friend? What can have brought you to this unhappy end?"

"Talking brought me here," replied the head. "Talking brought me to this place."

Mbundu people, south-west Africa

Princess Gumbi's Song

From *King Gumbi and His Lost Daughter*

List, all you men,
To the song I sing.
I am Gumbi's child,
Brought up in the wild;
And home I return,
As you all will learn,
When this my little drum
Tells Gumbi I have come, come, come.

I am Gumbi's child,
Make way for me;
I am homeward bound,
Make way for me.

Manyema people, the Congo

Song for Saada

From *The Story of Liongo*

O thou handmaid Saada, list my words today!
Haste thee to my mother, tell her what I say.
Bid her bake for me a cake of chaff and bran, I pray,
And hide therein an iron file to cut my bonds away,
File to free my fettered feet, swiftly as I may;
Forth I'll glide like serpent's child, silently to slay.

Swahili-speaking peoples, east Africa
✤

Binti Ali's Song

From *Binti Ali the Clever*

Makami, behold my bracelets and rings.
See my anklets, Makami. Aha, behold!
See the chain for my neck of beautiful gold.
Behold now my ear-rings and nose-stud see.
Lola, Makami, lola, look well at me.
I'm Binti Ali, the Wazir's daughter;
I came, Makami, from over the water.
We are seven in all, the last born am I.
Farewell, Makami, for I bid you goodbye.
Lola, Makami, lola, farewell.

Swahili-speaking peoples, east Africa
❀

Olokun's Revenge

After he had lived among the human race for a long period of time, Obatala came to the decision that he had done all he could for his people. The day had arrived for him to retire, he believed, and so he climbed up the golden chain and returned to his home in the sky once more, promising to visit the earth as frequently as possible. The other gods never tired of hearing Obatala describe the kingdom he had created below. Many were so captivated by the image he presented of the newly created human beings, that they decided to depart from the sky and go down to live among them. And as they prepared to leave, Olorun took them aside and counselled them:

"Each of you shall have a special role while you are down there, and I ask that you never forget your duty to the human race. Always listen to the prayers of the people and offer help when they are in need."

One deity, however, was not at all pleased with Obatala's work or the praise he had received from Olorun. The goddess Olokun, ruler of the sea, watched with increasing fury as, one by one, the other gods arrived in her domain and began dividing up the land amongst themselves.

"Obatala has never once consulted me about any of this," she announced angrily, "but he shall pay for the insult to my honour."

The goddess commanded the great waves of her ocean to rise up, for it was her intention to destroy the land Obatala had created and replace it with water once more. The terrible ood began, and soon the elds were completely submerged. Crops were destroyed and thousands of people were swept away by the roaring tide.

Those who survived the deluge ed to the hills and called to Obatala for help, but he could not hear them from his home high above in the sky.

In desperation, the people turned to Eshu, one of the gods recently descended to earth.

"Please return to the sky," they begged, "and tell the great gods of the ood that threatens to destroy everything."

"First you must show that you revere the gods," replied Eshu. "You must offer up a sacri ce and pray hard that you will be saved."

The people went away and returned with a goat which they sacri ced as food for Obatala. But still Eshu refused to carry the message.

"You ask me to perform this great service," he told them, "and yet you do not offer to reward me. If I am to be your messenger, I too deserve a gift."

The people offered up more sacri ces to Eshu and only when he was content that they had shown him appropriate respect did he begin to climb the golden chain back to the sky to deliver his message.

Obatala was deeply upset by the news and extremely anxious for the safety of his people, for he was uncertain how best to deal with so powerful a goddess as Olokun. Once more, he approached Orunmila and asked for advice. Orunmila consulted his divining nuts, and at last he said to Obatala:

"Rest here in the sky while I descend below. I will use my gifts to turn back the water and make the land rise again." Orunmila went down and, using his special powers, brought the waves under control so that the marshes began to dry up and land became visible again. But although the people greeted the god as their saviour and pleaded with him to act as their protector, Orunmila confessed that he had no desire to remain among them. Before he departed, however, he passed on a great many of his gifts to the people, teaching them how to divine the future and to control the unseen forces of nature. What he taught the people was never lost and it was passed on like a precious heirloom from one generation to another.

Yoroba people, west Africa

The Song of Kwege

From *Kwege and Bahati*

I, Kwege, weep, I weep!
And my crying is what the birds say.
Oh, you log, my tabu!
I cry in the speech of the birds.
They have taken my clothes,
They have taken my leglets,
They have taken my beads,
I am turned into Bahati.
Bahati is turned into Kwege.
I weep in the speech of the birds.

Zaramo people, Tanzania

The Jackal and the Spring

Once upon a time all the streams and rivers ran so dry that the animals did not know how to get water. After a very long search, which had been quite in vain, they found a tiny spring, which only wanted to be dug deeper so as to yield plenty of water. So the beasts said to each other, "Let us dig a well, and then we shall not fear to die of thirst;" and they all consented except the jackal, who hated work of any kind, and generally got somebody to do it for him.

When they had nished their well, they held a council as to who should be made the guardian of the well, so that the jackal might not come near it, for, they said, "he would not work, therefore he shall not drink."

After some talk it was decided that the rabbit should be left in charge; then all the other beasts went back to their homes.

When they were out of sight the jackal arrived. "Good morning! Good morning, rabbit!" and the rabbit politely said, "Good morning!" Then the jackal unfastened the little bag that hung at his side, and pulled out of it a piece of honeycomb which he began to eat, and turning to the rabbit he remarked:

"As you see, rabbit, I am not thirsty in the least, and this is nicer than any water." "Give me a bit," asked the rabbit. So the jackal handed him a very little morsel. "Oh, how good it is!" cried the rabbit; "give me a little more, dear friend!" But the jackal answered, "If you really want me to give you some more, you must have your paws tied behind you, and lie on your back, so that I can pour it into your mouth."

The rabbit did as he was bid, and when he was tied tight and popped on his back, the jackal ran to the spring and drank as much as he wanted. When he had quite nished he returned to his den.

In the evening the animals all came back, and when they saw the rabbit lying with his paws tied, they said to him: "Rabbit, how did you let yourself be taken in like this?"

"It was all the fault of the jackal," replied the rabbit; "he tied me up like this, and told me he would give me something nice to eat. It was all a trick just to get at our water."

"Rabbit, you are no better than an idiot to have let the jackal drink our water when he would not help to nd it. Who shall be our next watchman? We must have somebody a little sharper than you!" and the little hare called out, "I will be the watchman."

The following morning the animals all went their various ways, leaving the little hare to guard the spring. When they were out of sight the jackal came back. "Good morning! good morning, little hare," and the little hare politely said, "Good morning."

"Can you give me a pinch of snuff?" said the jackal. "I am so sorry, but I have none," answered the little hare. The jackal then came and sat down by the little hare, and unfastened his little bag, pulling out of it a piece of honeycomb. He licked his lips and exclaimed, "Oh, little hare, if you only knew how good it is!"

"What is it?" asked the little hare.

"It is something that moistens my throat so deliciously," answered the jackal, "that after I have eaten it I don't feel thirsty anymore, while I am sure that all you other beasts are forever wanting water."

"Give me a bit, dear friend," asked the little hare.

"Not so fast," replied the jackal. "If you really wish to enjoy what you are eating, you must have your paws tied behind you, and lie on your back, so that I can pour it into your mouth."

"You can tie them, only be quick," said the little hare, and when he was tied tight and popped on his back, the jackal went quietly down to the well, and drank as much as he wanted. When he had quite nished he returned to his den. In the evening the animals all came back; and when they saw the little hare with his paws tied, they said to him: "Little hare, how did you let yourself be taken in like this? Didn't you boast you were very sharp? You undertook to guard our water; now show us how much is left for us to drink!"

"It is all the fault of the jackal," replied the little hare, "He told me he would give me something nice to eat if I would just let him tie my hands behind my back."

Then the animals said, "Who can we trust to mount guard now?" And the panther answered, "Let it be the tortoise." The following morning the animals all went their various ways, leaving the tortoise to guard the spring. When they were out of sight the jackal came back. "Good morning, tortoise; good morning."

But the tortoise took no notice. "Good morning, tortoise; good morning." But still the tortoise pretended not to hear. Then the jackal said to himself, "Well, today I have only got to manage a bigger idiot than before. I shall just kick him on one side, and then go and have a drink." So he went up to the tortoise and said to him in a soft voice, "Tortoise! tortoise!" but the tortoise took no notice. Then the jackal kicked him out of the way, and went to the well and began to drink, but scarcely had he touched the water, than the tortoise seized him by the leg. The jackal shrieked out: "Oh, you will break my leg!" but the tortoise only held on the tighter. The jackal then took his bag and tried to make the tortoise smell the honeycomb he had inside; but the tortoise turned away his head and smelt nothing. At last the jackal said to the tortoise, "I should like to give you my bag and everything in it," but the only answer the tortoise made was to grasp the jackal's leg tighter still.

So matters stood when the other animals came back. The moment he saw them, the jackal gave a violent tug, and managed to free his leg, and then took to his heels as fast as he could. And the animals all said to the tortoise:

"Well done, tortoise, you have proved your courage; now we can drink from our well in peace, as you have got the better of that thieving jackal!"

from southern Africa

Tortoises Hunting Ostriches

One day, it is said, the Tortoises held a council how they might hunt Ostriches, and they said, "Let us, on both sides, stand in rows near each other, and let one go to hunt the Ostriches, so that they must ee along through the midst of us."

They did so, and as they were many, the Ostriches were obliged to run along through the midst of them. During this they did not move, but, remaining always in the same places, called each to the other, "Are you there?" and each one answered, "I am here." The Ostriches hearing this, ran so tremendously that they quite exhausted their strength, and fell down. Then the Tortoises assembled by-and-by at the place where the Ostriches had fallen, and devoured them.

from southern Africa

CELEBRATIONS
& PRAYERS

Raindrops (The Prayer)

Allahmdillulah
I feel raindrops on my shoulders.
I feel raindrops on my head.

Oh kind king, Won't you save me, please?
I don't want to be another maybe I
n the book you revealed me!
So, possibly, If you're listening,
I need a hero.

Not some prince on a white horse,
If that's the case, you might as well turn me to a corpse
Back to dust
Because I lack the basic concept of trust
And…
I'm looking for a hero!

Not Superman!
He's too enchanted with Louis,
Too human for me!
It's my spirit that's crying,

It's my spirit that's dying!

It used to be my heart aching but lately,

I'm struggling to fight the numbness as the voices get louder

Threatening me with all their powers!

Oh Kind King!

I've heard wondrous tales about you filled you

    with magic miracles!

I hear you can wash me white as snow.

Make me beautiful inside like you;

Brand new on the day you rose

To those gold streets we all long to see!

Kind King,

I don't want to be a maybe.

I'm a mere mortal;

Broken at one end hoping that one day

The darkness will fade.

But I need saving,

Lots of love and no mysteries

I feel raindrops on my shoulders.
I feel raindrops on my head.
Allahmdillulah

Ndi'Aphrykah

IN PRAISE OF AHMADA (EXTRACT)

Let us thank the everlasting God
Praise be to the King who created Muhammad.
Let us for ever invoke blessings and peace
Upon the Prophet who excels all others, Ahmada.
Accept, oh people, let us praise Ahmada.
God has enjoined us to praise him
Let us make firm our intention to praise Muhammad.
That we might obtain light and radiance of heart
And be cleansed by praising the Finest One.
We beg forgiveness from God who is instant
 in His Generosity,
May he give it to us because of the rank of Ahmada.
We pray for pardon that He might forgive us
The Munificent King, for the sake of Ahmada.
The best of the best he excels every other rank
God himself who said that He has raised Ahmada
 above all others.
The heavens are limitless, but they do not reach
As high as the glory of Muhammad.
The glory of the firmament seems diminished
 when compared to

The glory of our Prophet Muhammad.

His light exceeds the light of the full moon

There is no light like the light of Muhammad.

As for bravery, no warrior has ever matched the
  courage shown by Ahmada.

Musk and myrrh do not equal

The perfume emitted by the body of Muhammad.

As for his beauty and physique, he surpassed all

For nowhere is there the like of Muhammad.

There has never been created a man like him

Cheerful and smiling was Muhammad.

Nana Asma'u (1793–1864)

So Verily (extract)

Lord God Almighty, all Powerful, he who asserts
     there is more
than one God will perish.
One God, Almighty, nothing is perfect except
     it comes from Him.
Come to God, receive His generosity: all good things
     are derived from him.
Anyone who says he requires nothing of God is either
     ignorant or an unbeliever.
Everyone who seeks God's help will receive it,
for God allows people to make requests.
I pray God will show me the Way of religion and that
     I will keep to it until I die.
God is pure, and forgets nothing: those who forgive
     find peace.
May He bless us and show us the path and may
     He help us to remain one people.
We pray for victory and that the rebellion of Ibra
     may be overcome.
We pray too, for forgiveness in this world and in the next.

Call upon God always, so that things which are too
   difficult may be made easy.
Pray to God, do your meditations, praying for forgiveness
   and giving thanks.
Look at His generosity! It is unbounded, His munificence
   is infinite.
We give thanks to God and pray for our Lord
   of the Universe.

Nana Asma'u (1793–1864)

HOME, SWEET HOME

Sharers of a common country,
They had met in deadly strife;
Men who should have been as brothers
Madly sought each other's life.

In the silence of the even,
When the cannon's lips were dumb,
Thoughts of home and all its loved ones
To the soldier's heart would come.

On the margin of a river,
'Mid the evening's dews and damps,
Could be heard the sounds of music
Rising from two hostile camps.

One was singing of its section
Down in Dixie, Dixie's land,
And the other of the banner
Waved so long from strand to strand.

In the land where Dixie's ensign
Floated o'er the hopeful slave,
Rose the song that freedom's banner,
Starry-lighted, long might wave.

From the fields of strife and carnage,
Gentle thoughts began to roam,
And a tender strain of music
Rose with words of "Home, Sweet Home."

Then the hearts of strong men melted,
For amid our grief and sin
Still remains that "touch of nature,"
Telling us we all are kin.

In one grand but gentle chorus,
Floating to the starry dome,
Came the words that brought them nearer,
Words that told of "Home, Sweet Home."

For awhile, all strife forgotten,
They were only brothers then,
Joining in the sweet old chorus,
Not as soldiers, but as men.

Men whose hearts would flow together,
Though apart their feet might roam,
Found a tie they could not sever,
In the mem'ry of each home.

Never may the steps of carnage
Shake our land from shore to shore,
But may mother, home and Heaven,
Be our watchwords evermore.

Frances Harper (1825–1911)
⌘

BROWN LEGS

My friend's legs are brown,
Don't get me wrong.
Not any ordinary brown,
They are luminous,
She is only ever so superficially sunburnt,
Black men stare at her legs as if they were trapped,
Arrested by anomaly,
Those almost white legs on a black woman?
Hooogh!
Even you,
Wouldn't you want some of that almost, almost?

She's no dum dum.
She knows…
She wears short skirts,
Hoisted high,
Sits on bar stools,
Flawless caramel legs crossed,
When I go out with her,
I know I'm screwed,
Even dressed like a peacock,

Cleavage slipping down to my navel,
I won't get any male attention.

Soon a gaggle of guys gathers,
I skulk,
The scented aroma of her high-pitched giggle
Wafts under my nose,
She knows how to play.
Now she's a white chick,
She laughs at jamaa's stale jokes.

Meanwhile I sit darkly alone
Nurse my cool drink,
Pretend not to care.

Sitawa Namwalie

Was I Ever?

Was I ever like that?
Like that!
My shoulders, a wide expanse
A shape of certainty so straight and firm?
Was I like that, ever?
My hips an unasked question mark
In search of insolence and answers
When I walked you by?

Did young men slide me looks
From under lingering eyes
And then simply smile?
Did old men follow me with brazen stares
And then deeply sigh?

Was I ever like that?
Like that!
My skin a promised challenge,
Bronzed, firm, soft
All at the same time?

Did I too walk with cruel *insouciance*,
Flashing teeth and careless pride?
Did I leave men breathing sharply
As I passed them shapely by?

Was I ever?
Was I like that?
Like that!
When I too was young?

Sitawa Namwalie

SWIM

On the day you were born it rained.
Grandmother carried you in a cloth
over her chest to the river.
The child must learn to swim, she said.
Her limbs must flex against the tide
her lungs must create room for water
she must learn to drown.
She approached the bank and removed her cloth
bore her naked flesh to the river with the women
of our village behind her,

        a dozen eyes towards God.

They called on Twieduampon Kwame,
the giver of life and destiny to bring you peace –
from the tirade of tongues peppered with insults for
women like you.
She laid you flat in the arms of the river
beckoning the spirits of ancestors to follow you.
She knew, that your path was set for a land
destined to bring you more confusion than harmony.
The women drew towards the water and each
extended a hand towards you,

a ring of apology and promise.
From every home, every street corner, every hut
came whispered prayers.
They gave thanks for the voice you would have.
The freedom you would wear loosely.
The pride you would bring back and the stories of culture,
legacy, and courage you would take of the women
who extended a hand.
The women wearing your skin,
their reflection in your eyes,
their voice in your vernacular.
For them, you would become a living tribute,
a testament to how we live.

Tina Abena Oforiwa

A Hymn

When morn awakes our hearts
To pour the matin prayer;
When toil-worn day departs,
And gives a pause to care;
When those our souls love best
Kneel with us, in Thy fear,
To ask Thy peace and rest—
O God, our Father, hear!

When worldly snares without,
And evil thoughts within,
Stir up some impious doubt,
Or lure us back to sin;
When human strength proves frail,
And will but half sincere;
When faith begins to fail—
O God, our Father, hear!

When in our cup of mirth
The drop of trembling falls,
And the frail props of earth

Are crumbling around our walls;
When back we gaze with grief,
And forward glance with fear,
When faileth man's relief—
O God, our father, hear!

When on the verge we stand
Of the eternal clime,
And Death with solemn hand
Draws back the veil of Time;
When flesh and spirit quake
Before three to appear—
For the redeemer's sake,
O God, our Father, hear!

Thomas Pringle

Mozambican Mystery

Last night I died in Casablanca
And found my heart in Malawi
I watched the stars in Madagascar
And sailed across the Galilee.

I walked the fields in Mozambique
And climbed the hills of Tennessee
I caught the sun in Buenos Aires
And chased the moon in Sicily.

I met the Rose of Spanish Harlem
We danced all night in Tripoli
She followed me across the ocean
And we made love from dawn till three.

I was reborn in Abu Dhabi
I found my soul in Waikiki
Tonight I'll sleep in Costa Rica
And live a life that's winter free.

Harold Lee Rush

THE PRAYER

Talk not of prayers that fail; the prayers unheard
Are not the askings Paul meant when he said:
"Pray without ceasing." Be thou well assured,
The true petition, not of barren word,
But plumed of deed, scales Heaven overheard,
Where souls and suns from God's high throne are shed.
Pray without ceasing, let good deeds unfold
Like petals of a rose, until, complete,
The flower of asking, full and fair and sweet,
Is fit for God's right hand to take and hold.
False prayers are barren breath, like vapour rolled
Between men and the stars; they hide the feet
Of angels. But the prayer, wise and meet,
From chiming sphere to sphere on high is told.

W.C. Scully

AN HYMN TO THE MORNING

Attend my lays, ye ever honour'd nine,
Assist my labours, and my strains refine;
In smoothest numbers pour the notes along,
For bright Aurora now demands my song.

Aurora hail, and all the thousand dies,
Which deck thy progress through the vaulted skies:
The morn awakes, and wide extends her rays,
On ev'ry leaf the gentle zephyr plays;

Harmonious lays the feather'd race resume,
Dart the bright eye, and shake the painted plume.
Ye shady groves, your verdant gloom display
To shield your poet from the burning day:

Calliope awake the sacred lyre,
While thy fair sisters fan the pleasing fire:
The bow'rs, the gales, the variegated skies
In all their pleasures in my bosom rise.

See in the east th' illustrious king of day!
His rising radiance drives the shades away—

But Oh! I feel his fervid beams too strong,
And scarce begun, concludes th' abortive song.

Phillis Wheatley (c. 1753–84)

Hymn 1083

From *The Life, History, and Unparalleled Sufferings of John Jea, the African Preacher. Compiled and Written by Himself*

We part in body, not in mind;
Our minds continue one;
And each to each in Jesus join'd,
We hand in hand go on.

Subsists as in us all one soul,
No power can make us twain;
And mountains rise and oceans roll,
To sever us in vain.

Present we still in spirit are,
And intimately nigh;
While on the wings of faith and prayer,
We each to other fly.

In Jesus Christ together we
In heavenly places sit:
Cloth'd with the sun, we smile to see
The moon beneath our feet.

Our life is hid with Christ in God:
Our life shall soon appear,
And shed his glory all abroad,
In all his members here.

The heavenly treasure now we have
In a vile house of clay:
But he shall to the utmost save,
And keep us to that day.

Our souls are in his mighty hand,
And he shall keep them still;
And you and I shall surely stand
With him on Sion's hill!

Him eye to eye we there shall see;
Our face like his shall shine:
O what a glorious company,
When saints and angels join!

O what a joyful meeting there!
In robes of white array'd,
Palms in our hands we all shall bear
And crowns upon our head.

Then let us lawfully contend,
And fight our passage through;
Bear in our faithful minds the end,
And keep the prize in view.

Then let us hasten to the day,
When all shall be brought home!
Come, O Redeemer, come away!
O Jesus, quickly come!

God of all consolation, take
The glory of thy grace!
Thy gifts to thee we render back,
In ceaseless songs of praise.

Thro' thee we now together came,
In singleness of heart;
We met, O Jesus, in thy name,
And in thy name we part.

John Jea (born 1773)

The Feast

Once there lived a kind and generous chief who wished
to repay his people for the long hours they had worked
for him on his farm. An idea came to him that he should
hold a great feast and so he sent messengers to all of
the surrounding villages inviting the men, women and
children to attend his home the following evening,
asking only that each man bring a calabash of wine along
to the celebrations.

Next day, there was great excitement among the people.
They chatted noisily about the event as they worked in the
fields and when they had finished their labour they returned
home to bathe and dress themselves in their finest robes.
By sunset, more than a hundred men and their families
lined the roadside. They laughed happily as they moved
along, beating their drums and dancing in time to the
rhythm. When they arrived at the chief's compound, the
head of every household emptied his calabash into a large
earthenware pot that stood in the centre of the courtyard.
Soon the pot was more than half full and they all looked
forward to their fair share of the refreshing liquid.

Among the chief's subjects there was a poor man who very much wanted to attend the feast, but he had no wine to take to the festivities and was too proud to appear empty-handed before his friends.

"Why don't you buy some wine from our neighbour?" his wife asked him, "he looks as though he has plenty to spare." "But why should we spend money on a feast that is free?" the poor man answered her. "No, there must be another way."

And after he had thought about it hard for a few minutes he turned to his wife and said:

"There will be a great many people attending this feast, each of them carrying a calabash of wine. I'm sure that if I added to the pot just one calabash of water, nobody would notice the difference."

His wife was most impressed by this plan, and while her husband went and filled his calabash with water, she stepped indoors and put on her best tunic and what little jewellery she possessed, delighted at the prospect of a good meal and an evening's free entertainment.

When the couple arrived at the chief's house they saw all the other guests empty the wine they had brought into the large earthen pot. The poor man moved forward nervously and followed their example. Then he went to where the men were gathered and sat down with them to await the serving of the wine.

As soon as the chief was satisfied that all the guests had arrived, he gave the order for his servants to begin filling everyone's bowl. The vessels were filled and the men looked to their host for the signal to begin the drinking. The poor man grew impatient, for he was quite desperate to have the taste of the wine on his lips, and could scarcely remember when he had last enjoyed such a pleasant experience for free.

At length, the chief stood up and delivered a toast to his people. Then he called for his guests to raise their bowls to their lips. Each of them tasted their wine, swallowed it, and waited to feel a warm glow inside.

They swallowed some more of the wine, allowing it to trickle slowly over their tongues, and waited for the flavour to release itself. But the wine tasted as plain as any water. And now, all around the room, the guests began to shuffle their feet and cough with embarrassment.

"This is really very good wine," one of the men spoke up eventually. "Indeed it is the best I've ever tasted," agreed another. "Quite the nest harvest I've ever come across," added his neighbour. But the chief of the people knew precisely what had happened, and he smiled at the comical spectacle as each man tried to hide the fact that he had filled his calabash that morning from the village spring. The enormous earthen pot contained nothing but water, and it was water that the people were given to drink at the chief's great feast. For the chief had very wisely decided in his own mind: "When only water is brought to the feast, water is all that should be served."

from Cameroon, west Africa

A Chant

From *The Village Maiden and the Cannibal*

The Water Spirit loves not the thin roots,
They are the food of swine –
There is no safety for them.
But the large root, how good it is –
It is the food of spirits, even of the
Great Water Spirit.
Safety and strength are in it;
The water flows on, flows on.

from Lesotho, southern Africa

PROTEST &
SURVIVAL

My Legs Are in Mourning

My legs are in mourning today, and almost all week.
Adorned with dark colors inside and out
And the agony they endure at the initial shock,
    until the pain gradually fades away.
The stress is felt at their head and center – a dull and
    pulsating sensation that comes and goes, as if something
    is being stripped from the inside,
As if something is being squeezed from the inside.
And everything about me changes; all is affected by this
death of life, of freedom,
Until comfort returns.

Their sleep shall be restless tonight and for some nights
    to come,
Until the crying lessens and the tears begin to dry.
But the tears they cry are red, and they come from
    a single eye.
Yes, they bleed for those whom they mourn; they don't
    just cry; they weep.
This is no superficial mourning.

And pleasure shall be forsaken and denied

For enjoyment cannot be had while mourning,

And their state will be recognized by all

For the colors of mourning are black and red and dark blue,

Colors that can hide the tears if they decide to show.

But soon, the tears will flow clear and few.

And my legs, they will act with care and restraint,

> for this is no time to be normal.

They cannot be normal no matter how hard they try, or

how much they pretend, or how deep they hide.

A force beyond them has gripped them.

Somberness has taken over.

Sometimes they double up in pain, but that state is soon over.

And sometimes they cannot keep still out of fear

> of the unspeakable

Until the mourning period is done, and they can don

> their light colors.

Until the mourning period is over, and they can do

> what they used to do.

It has happened before (not too long ago)

And it will happen again (soon)

My legs are in mourning today, and almost all week.

Kafui Adjaye-Gbewonyo

PURSUIT OF HAPPYNESS

I have spent countless hours
At church,
Pubs
And strip clubs.
With pastors,
Prostitutes
And drunkards.
In pursuit of happyness,
The truth
And fleshly desires.
Sang happy songs with Hedonists
Travelled with Nomads,
Got high with Rastas
And broke bread with Pariahs.
Camped on bended knees around hell-like fires
To listen attentively to grown men liars.

Slaughtered sheep,
Goats
And cows
For this little bit of sanity

And crowded peace of mind,
But my hands are smeared with blood
And the dark cloud still looms closely behind
Where the hell is this love?
I only know hearts for pumping blood.
Not as an asylum for
Said feelings you people cannot even describe.

And do you remember
When god said "let there be light!"?
I was unfortunate
And cast out
To write this poem
With my tongue in the grim dark
I am convinced collecting empty beer bottles
And picking bread crumbs is my birth right.
I am still in hot pursuit
And the journey now leads me
To a mad house.

Azola Dayile

Go Work in My Vineyard

Go work in my vineyard, said the Lord,
And gather the bruised grain;
But the reapers had left the stubble bare,
And I trod the soil in pain.

The fields of my Lord are wide and broad,
He has pastures fair and green,
And vineyards that drink the golden light
Which flows from the sun's bright sheen.

I heard the joy of the reapers' song,
As they gathered golden grain;
Then wearily turned unto my task,
With a lonely sense of pain.

Sadly I turned from the sun's fierce glare,
And sought the quiet shade,
And over my dim and weary eyes
Sleep's peaceful fingers strayed.

I dreamed I joined with a restless throng,
Eager for pleasure and gain;
But ever and anon a stumbler fell,
And uttered a cry of pain.

But the eager crowd still hurried on,
Too busy to pause or heed,
When a voice rang sadly through my soul,
You must staunch these wounds that bleed.

My hands were weak, but I reached them out
To feebler ones than mine,
And over the shadows of my life
Stole the light of a peace divine.

Oh! then my task was a sacred thing,
How precious it grew in my eyes!
'Twas mine to gather the bruised grain
For the "Lord of Paradise."

And when the reapers shall lay their grain
On the floors of golden light,
I feel that mine with its broken sheaves
Shall be precious in His sight.

Though thorns may often pierce my feet,
And the shadows still abide,
The mists will vanish before His smile,
There will be light at eventide.

Frances Harper (1825–1911)

The Life, History and Unparalleled Sufferings of John Jea (Extract)

I, John Jea, the subject of this narrative, was born in the town of Old Callabar, in Africa, in the year 1773. My father's name was Hambleton Robert Jea, my mother's name Margaret Jea; they were of poor, but industrious parents. At two years and a half old, I and my father, mother, brothers, and sisters, were stolen, and conveyed to North America, and sold for slaves; we were then sent to New York, the man who purchased us was very cruel, and used us in a manner, almost too shocking to relate; my master and mistress's names were Oliver and Angelika Triebuen, they had seven children – three sons and four daughters; he gave us a very little food or raiment, scarcely enough to satisfy us in any measure whatever; our food was what is called Indian corn pounded or bruised and boiled with water, the same way burgo is made, and about a quart of sour butter-milk poured on it; for one person two quarts of this mixture, and about three ounces of dark bread, per day, the bread was darker than that usually allowed to convicts, and greased over with very indifferent hog's lard; at other times when he was better pleased, he would allow us about half-a-pound of beef for a week, and about half-a-gallon of potatoes; but that was very seldom the case, and yet we esteemed ourselves better used than many of our neighbours.

Our labour was extremely hard, being obliged to work in the summer from about two o'clock in the morning, till about ten or eleven o'clock at night, and in the winter from four in the morning, till ten at night. The horses usually rested about five hours in the day, while we were at work; thus did the beasts enjoy greater privileges than we did. We dared not murmur, for if we did we were corrected with a weapon an inch and-a-half thick, and that without mercy, striking us in the most tender parts, and if we complained of this usage, they then took four large poles, placed them in the ground, tied us up to them, and flogged us in a manner too dreadful to behold; and when taken down, if we offered to lift up our hand or foot against our master or mistress, they used us in a most cruel manner; and often they treated the slaves in such a manner as caused their death, shooting them with a gun, or beating their brains out with some weapon, in order to appease their wrath, and thought no more of it than if they had been brutes: this was the general treatment which slaves experienced. After our master had been treating us in this cruel manner, we were obliged to thank him for the punishment he had been inflicting on us, quoting that Scripture which saith, "Bless the rod, and him that hath appointed it." But, though he was a professor of religion, he forgot that passage which saith "God is love, and whoso dwelleth in love dwelleth in God, and God in him." And, again, we are commanded to love our enemies; but it appeared evident that his wretched heart was hardened; which led us to look up unto him as our god, for we did not know him who is able to deliver and save all who call upon him in truth and sincerity. Conscience, that faithful monitor, (which either excuses or accuses) caused us to groan, cry, and sigh, in a manner which cannot be uttered.

We were often led away with the idea that our masters were our gods; and at other times we placed our ideas on the sun, moon, and stars, looking unto them, as if they could save us; at length we found, to our great disappointment, that these were nothing else but the works of the Supreme Being; this caused me to wonder how my master frequently expressed that all his houses, land, cattle, servants, and every thing which he possessed was his own; not considering that it was the Lord of Hosts, who has said that the gold and the silver, the earth, and the fullness thereof, belong to him.

Our master told us, that when we died, we should be like the beasts that perish; not informing us of God, heaven, or eternal punishments, and that God hath promised to bring the secrets of every heart into judgment, and to judge every man according to his works.

From the following instances of the judgments of God, I was taught that he is God, and there is none besides him, neither in the heavens above, nor in the earth beneath, nor in the waters under the earth; for he doth with the armies of heaven and the inhabitants of the earth as seemeth him good; and there is none that can stay his hand, nor say unto him, with a prevailing voice, what dost thou?

My master was often disappointed in his attempts to increase the produce of his lands; for oftentimes he would command us to carry out more seed into the field to insure a good crop, but when it sprang up and promised to yield plentifully, the Almighty caused the worms to eat it at the root, and destroyed nearly the whole produce; God thus showing him his own inability to preserve the fruits of the earth.

John Jea (born 1773)

They Walk Among Us

They walk among us
feeding on our love and kindness
thirsting for our love

They lay hungry on a bed of passion
with their hearts ajar
uncertainty creeps into their hearts' little cracks
bathed in love yet dry with anxiety
you questioned their hearts
but they answered with fears
their insecurities bathed in frostiness.

They live among us
feeding on our kindness
thirsting for our love

They dream in music but the sleep on thorns
poisonous arrows pass through their hearts
stung by fear for passion
fleshed ripped with insecurity
they walk a crooked line of broken dreams

murmuring cold whispers that bring doubts
their silent symphony so loud

They breathe among us
feeding on our kindness
thirsting for our love

Fountain of tears stream down their cheeks
choked by emotion no words can they speak
caged around walls of darkness
obsessive uncertainty blinding their souls
their skin tightened around their eyes
sweat beading screening truth
not knowing right from wrong

They lie among us
feeding on our kindness
thirsting for our love

Our unconditional love never satisfies them
our tender embraces never warm enough

our lonely cries never move them
Greed ripping through their bodies
The teeth of uncertainty
clench and grind around them
like steel claws on slate they cling to their hearts
with a sharpened hold turmoil strike on them
their caged cold hearts refusing to let us in
shutting us out beyond death
only cold air within their clasp

Whenever we reach out
We find nothing for our hands to touch
realizing the sudden bland flavour of our lives
no longer drawing out our breath
we drown us in their pool of sorrow
puncturing into our spine
grimly drilling holes through

Yes, they are indeed among us
calling us friends
lovers

companions

promising to be there

but only to feed on our sadness.

Like the raging fire intense emotions well up

Shrinking their souls as they penetrate

The coldness of their souls stinging us

With shuddered grasp we pull back

Clutching our hearts they wrench them out

Stomping on our trust like yesterdays trash

Angels cry as innocent souls they crush

Life of the innocent drain out

Wasted, spent, lost, wrung

droplets of red staining the soil

taking us on a rollercoaster of pain

burrowing into our flesh

tenaciously ripping tunnels through

Yes, they live among us.

terrified and alone

terrified of their spirits

terrified of their choices
hiding behind hardness
hiding from the truth
not knowing there to turn
not trusting themselves
not sure of their future.

They feed on crushing our love
choking our laughter
they breathe on perforating our lives
feeding on our kindness
they walk among us
thirsting for our love

Sandra A. Mushi

HARGEYSA

I came to you the first time pretending
    I could understand,
figure you out, cup your soul in my hand, map it,
    and sell it.
Tarmac roads and electronics shops slapped
    my empty hand.

The streets bathed in women's gorgora
vivid like Joseph's coat multiplied.
Plastic bags in yellow, pink, blue, fluttered
like nests in the thorn bushes,
filled with ghosts of birds long-fled.
Strawberry and blue ice cream walls:
could I help dreaming in colour?
My eyes closed against fine sand.
Very firmly against begging children
and makeshift hovels close to Parliament.

I know this time
that this is a place you come to listen
to the sound of hues, of wind-driven grit,
of bullets and weddings in the night;

to hear the story of the MIG trapped in time.
And see the power of the Somali woman.

One day I might begin to know.

Phyllis Muthoni

MAKING THE CUT

(There are things we fight to forget that will haunt us forever)

Between your legs was a burning highway
smouldering lava oozing down your thighs.
He will later try to hold you, caress the spot
    and you will hate him.

Amina said it was worse than pulling teeth,
mouth gargling blood, eyes rolling back and finally a
blackout.

For days, your father's face will emanate a radiant awe.
The women of your house will congregate around your bed
and speak of your bravery.
Each face will look like a betrayal.

Your mother's eyes will avoid yours.
Your face will be an open terrain of vile discourse.
You will not hide your pain but wail till the ghost of her
own wound is reopened.

But they chant that you are pure.
That hollow well will never be a minefield to set men off, it
will be quiet.

Doused in the memory of this day it will hide.
Wait.
Close the door.
Light a match and if he dares, set him on fire.

Tina Abena Oforiwa

Natural Woman

When was the last time you felt the warm scalp of a woman
Run your fingers through her hair
Twisted her natural locks through your fingers
Or walked your fingers through the rows of braids
Just like walking through fields of corn

When did you see the true beauty of your African Woman?
Or saw a flawless dark skin?
Or kissed her natural plump lips?

From the days of slavery black women were told
    "You gotta have hair like 'Massa',
Don't want no nappy haired black as sin gal in the house"
The beautiful black women were kept in the cotton fields
While those that had lighter skin,
The products of the slave master s were kept as house slaves
If your hair was long and straight, without a natural
    crinkle it was your bonus,
a passport to heaven,
a ticket to the illusion of freedom

Now, I hardly see an original black woman

They all seem to have become Chinese, Indian and European

Flicking about hair that is not their own

That may be from a horse, a yak or plastic factory

Afraid to show their natural beauty

Afraid because their men have been conditioned to think

that a perfect woman has straight hair and fair skin

Afraid because their sisters would laugh and tease

them for their tight curls

Wake up!

Have you ever really looked at the beauty of a black

woman, all natural and dark?

They way her teeth and eyes sparkle in contrast to her skin

The way her hair feels soft like the ends of an ear of corn

Or woolly like that of a new born lamb

Twisting and curling itself through your fingers

True feelings exploding through the shaft of natural hair

Men! Treat a natural woman with respect

Women! rise up for the natural woman who dared

For her inner strength and inner pride have made

her able to go against the norm

To show her true self

Just the way God made her
Perfect
A beautiful black woman

Mariska Taylor-Darko
ꗋ

YOU WORK FOR ME

You work for me.
And I'm tired of seeing, my country men bleeding
for the sake of your fees.
See, you work for me,
But I can not believe in your incompetent grinning,
at my nations needs.
You work for me
inadequately.
Selfishly stabbing our unity.
Spitting at the beauty in diversity.
Disrespectfully rubbing dirt in the wounds which it should be,
your duty to heal for our children's prosperity.
Don't we drive on the same roads?
you'd rather take on loans?
Or aren't you here too?

Do you work for me?
Not the other way round?
When you mess up, its your job to with shame,
face the ground.
To get up and run, when any warning bells sound.

Not measure your cocks for some heat beaten crowd.

You don't care what parties I go to,

Why should I care the other way round?

Which schools will you build?

Where and how?

Can't you feel the vibrations?

My lakes suffocation?

Cañ you see your reflection?

before we all drown?

You Work For Me.

Do your job!

Get it right!

My land is filled with resources, inspiring!

Do the job you've got now,

before you start applying,

for promotions, with notions,

of wasting more of my time.

You Work For Me.

In case you forgot it.

My anger is past the point where I lost it.
The time has now come.
To get real.
Or Forfeit.

Raya Wambui

TO THE HONOURABLE T.H. ESQ; ON THE DEATH OF HIS DAUGHTER

While deep you mourn beneath the cypress-shade
The hand of Death, and your dear daughter laid
In dust, whose absence gives your tears to flow,
And racks your bosom with incessant woe,

Let Recollection take a tender part,
Assuage the raging tortures of your heart,
Still the wild tempest of tumultuous grief,
And pour the heav'nly nectar of relief:

Suspend the sigh, dear Sir, and check the groan,
Divinely bright your daughter's Virtues shone:
How free from scornful pride her gentle mind,
Which ne'er its aid to indigence declin'd!

Expanding free, it sought the means to prove
Unfailing charity, unbounded love!
She unreluctant flies to see no more
Her dear-lov'd parents on earth's dusky shore:

Impatient heav'n's resplendent goal to gain,
She with swift progress cuts the azure plain,
Where grief subsides, where changes are no more,
And life's tumultuous billows cease to roar;

She leaves her earthly mansion for the skies,
Where new creations feast her wond'ring eyes.
To heav'n's high mandate cheerfully resign'd
She mounts, and leaves the rolling globe behind;

She, who late wish'd that Leonard might return,
Has ceas'd to languish, and forgot to mourn;
To the same high empyreal mansions come,
She joins her spouse, and smiles upon the tomb:

And thus I hear her from the realms above:
"Lo! this the kingdom of celestial love!
"Could ye, fond parents, see our present bliss,
"How soon would you each sigh, each fear dismiss?

"Amidst unutter'd pleasures whilst I play

"In the fair sunshine of celestial day,

"As far as grief affects an happy soul

"So far doth grief my better mind controul,

"To see on earth my aged parents mourn,

"And secret wish for T——! to return:

"Let brighter scenes your ev'ning-hours employ:

"Converse with heav'n, and taste the promis'd joy."

Phillis Wheatley (c. 1753–84)

POET
BIOGRAPHIES

Kafui Adjaye-Gbewonyo

Kafui Adjaye-Gbewonyo is a Ghanaian-American public health professional. She has enjoyed writing poetry since childhood. Her poetic work has appeared in California State University, Bakersfield's literary journal, Orpheus. She was also recognized by the Live Poets Society of New Jersey as an American High School Poets Regional Winner in 2002 and was one of the recipients of the Edward Eager Memorial Fund Prize for Poetry at Harvard University in 2007.

Ndi'Aphrykah

Ndi'Aphrykah, born Morongoa Basadi Mosetlhi, is a young, Motswana writer, performing artist and entrepreneur. Her written works include poetry, short stories, novels and scripts. Through passion and determination, her artistic endeavours have provided her with numerous opportunities to expand her involvement and experience within the local arts industry.

She is currently working on an anthology and can be found on stage and behind-the-scenes at various local events. In future, she plans to continue writing and frequent international festivals as a performer.

Adjei Agyei Baah

Adjei is a lecturer, translator, editor and currently a PhD student at the University of Waikato, New Zealand. He is the co-founder of Africa Haiku Network, Poetry Foundation and the Mamba Journal, Africa's first international haiku journal. Adjei is a worldwide-anthologized poet and winner of several international awards. His maiden haiku collection *Afriku* was commended last year by Professor Wole Soyinka, Africa's first Nobel Prize Literature laureate. His other books are *Trio of Window*, *Ghana*, *21 Haiku* and *Piece Of My Fart*.

Azola Dayile

Azola Dayile is a writer and social activist from KwaZakhele, Port Elizabeth. He studied Journalism, Media and Philosophy at the Nelson Mandela University. Currently, he lives in Johannesburg where, besides trying to make ends meet, he thinks and writes for a living.

Tjawangwa Dema

Tjawangwa Dema is a Motswana poet, educator and arts administrator. Her collection *The Careless Seamstress* (University of Nebraska Press, 2019) won the Sillerman First Book Prize for African Poetry. Her chapbook *Mandible*

(Slapering Hol Press, 2014) was selected for the African Poetry Book Fund's New-Generation African Poets series. She has an MA in Creative Writing from Lancaster University and has given readings and taught workshops in over 20 countries. Her poems have been translated into languages including Spanish, Chinese, German and Swedish.

Gloria D. Gonsalves

Gloria D. Gonsalves, also fondly known as Auntie Glo, is an award-winning author and multi-published poet. Not just a writer, Gloria is a creative promoter for writing itself: she founded WoChiPoDa.com, an initiative aimed at instilling the love of poetry in young people. Her literary works aim to support humanitarian projects, inspire creativity, and impart moral and spiritual lessons. When taking a break from writing, she learns how to take lines for a walk. Find out more on her website: gloria-gonsalves.com

Sage Hassan

Sammy Sage Hassan is Nigeria and West Africa's premier poet. His face, voice and name was the persona of spoken word poetry in Nigeria when it first came into the attention of audiences. He has two poetry albums, over five videos that enjoyed flair play on major national stations, and a horde of newspaper, radio and TV appearances. Sage is an author of a few book, including *Dream Maker*. He writes for governments, organizations and people. He's an amateur filmmaker with two shorts to his credit, he lends his voice and face to film and stage; he is a teacher and life coach hoping to curate the wisdom and knowledge of all time for future generations.

Cynthia 'Flowchyld' Marangwanda

Cynthia Marangwanda is a poet, writer and blogger from Harare, Zimbabwe. She is an established spoken word poet who has been performing for over 10 years. Her influences include hip hop culture, urban life and the African experience. Her work deals with themes of African womanhood, decolonisation, indigenous spirituality, identity, the deconstruction of oppressive structures and transformation. She wrote the novella *Shards* in 2014, which won a national award for fiction in 2015. She has an honours degree in Women's and Gender Studies from Women's University in Africa.

Tinashe Mushakavanhu

Tinashe Mushakavanhu is a Zimbabwean poet. His current research on readingzimbabwe.com is a digital archive mapping the past 60 years of Zimbabwe's published history. He is a founding partner of Black Chalk & Co., a boutique agency engendering new forms of publishing and creative production. His forthcoming book, *Some Writers Can Give You Two Heartbeats*, is scheduled to appear in 2019. He holds a PhD in English from University of Kent, England.

Sandra A. Mushi

Sandra A. Mushi is an interior architecture designer with a very strong passion for writing. She is the author of *The Rhythmn Of My Rhyme* (Andika Afrika, Tanzania in 2008), a collection of soulful poems and a journey of self discovery – women in love; women out of love; abused children; abused women; content women; women who have found themselves (emotionally, mentally and sexually); and women who just want to be.

Phyllis Muthoni

Phyllis Muthoni is a poet, photographer (pmuthony.art), and editor, among other things. Her first collection of poetry, *Lilac Uprising*, has been likened to 'a cool drink of water: clear, spare, fresh and vital' (Doreen Baingana, author, *Tropical Fish*). 'Lilac Uprising', the title poem, is part of a four-piece poem that utilizes the life stages of a Jacaranda tree to highlight how she deals with the loss of her grandmother. She was a key contributor to Koroga, an online collaborative poetography project.

Sitawa Namwalie

Sitawa Namwalie is a Kenyan poet, playwright, writer and performer. She staged her first dramatized poetry show 'Cut Off My Tongue' in Nairobi in 2008 and published a book of the same name in 2009. 'Cut Off My Tongue' was invited to the UK's prestigious Hay Festival in the UK in 2009. Sitawa's second dramatized poetry performances include, 'Homecoming' (2011) and 'Silence is a Woman', which won Kenya's Sanaa Theatre Awards for Best Spoken Word and Poetry for her show of dramatized poetry.

Tina Abena Oforiwa

Tina Abena Oforiwa is a London-based, Ghanaian-born creative writer. Although she has lived in the UK almost all her life, for her, Ghana will always be home. Tina uses poetry as a means to communicate the experience of growing-up outside her homeland, the feeling of displacement and nostalgia which manifest in varying ways.

For Tina, poetry remains the ultimate liberating tool, it allows her to speak of things she wouldn't ordinarily engage with others about, feeling no reproach.

Yewande Omotoso

Yewande Omotoso is an architect, with a masters in creative writing from the University of Cape Town. Her debut novel 'Bomboy' (2011 Modjaji Books), won the South African Literary Award First Time Author Prize and was shortlisted for the Etisalat Prize for Literature. She was a 2015 Miles Morland Scholar. Yewande's second novel 'The Woman Next Door' (Chatto and Windus) was published in May 2016. It was shortlisted for the International Dublin Literary Award, the Aidoo-Snyder Prize, the Barry Ronge Fiction Prize, and the UJ Literary Prize. It was also longlisted for the Baileys Women's Literature Prize and was a finalist for the Hurston/Wright Legacy Awards for Fiction.

Harold Lee Rush

In 1982, Harold's broadcasting talents were discovered at Chicago's WGCI radio as the producer and co-host of the powerhouse morning show, where Rush created the 'Front Page' segment, which has been copied in morning shows across the country. In 2005 Rush worked at WKKC FM, the official radio station of the City Colleges of Chicago, as a Broadcast Instructor in the Media Communications Programs.

Tiro Sebina

Tiro Sebina teaches courses in Literary Theory and Criticism at University of Botswana. He also coordinates (UB) Writers' Workshop on Wednesday evenings. His poems appear in a number of anthologies and journals. He coaches Creative Writing on Friday afternoons at the Gaborone Public Library's Children's Section. Besides contributing occasional book reviews, he intermittently writes opinion columns in some newspapers in Botswana.

Mariska Taylor-Darko

Mariska Taylor-Darko is a widow with two sons. She is a writer, poet and motivational speaker. She is the founder of Yes Group Ghana, a motivational group involved in empowering the youth, and also an executive member of the Ghana Association of Writers. Mariska's poems have been featured several times on www.oneghanaonevoice. com, an online poetry site; in *Jambo*, an East African magazine; in a Spanish anthology titled *Ellas (Tambien) Cuentan;* and in other anthologies. She also has a book

titled *The Deer Hunt,* which is written around one poem of
the same title.

Janine 'Blaq Pearl' Van Rooy-Overmeyer

Janine 'Blaq Pearl' Van Rooy-Overmeyer, from Cape
Town, started writing poetry and songs at the age of 12.
Her musical genre is a fusion of Afro, Soul, Hip-hop, Jazz
and R&B. She is known for her phenomenal performances
at various events, national and international. Towards
the end of 2011 she finally released her debut album titled
Against All Odds. She is proudly vocal about social issues
and loves doing development work with youths. In 2015
she released *Karadaaa!!!* a collection of her poetry, stories
and songs written in both English and Afrikaans. She is the
co-founder of the Blaqpearl Foundation.

Raya Wambui

Raya Wambui started writing poetry consistently 19 years
ago. She began performing spoken word in 2011 and
launched her blog the next year, where she has been sharing
her poetry and journaling (rayawambui.com) ever since.
Her early poetry (in which 'You Work For Me' falls) is
characterized by passionately intimate candor.

Index